The • Life Cycle • Series

The Life Cycle of a

BAT

Rebecca Sjonger & Bobbie Kalman

Crabtree Publishing Company

www.crabtreebooks.com

The Life Cycle Series

A Bobbie Kalman Book

Dedicated by Heather Fitzpatrick
To my sisters and brother—Theresa, Sharon, Susan, Lenise, Sue-Anne, Sherri, and William

Editor-in-Chief
Bobbie Kalman

Writing team
Rebecca Sjonger
Bobbie Kalman

Substantive editor
Kelley MacAulay

Project editor
Robin Johnson

Editors
Molly Aloian
Reagan Miller
Kathryn Smithyman

Design
Margaret Amy Salter
Samantha Crabtree (cover)

Production coordinator
Heather Fitzpatrick

Photo research
Crystal Foxton

Consultant
Patricia Loesche, Ph.D., Animal Behavior Program,
Department of Psychology, University of Washington

Illustrations
Barbara Bedell: page 6
Cori Marvin: pages 5, 10
Bonna Rouse: back cover, pages 11, 14, 24

Photographs
Mark & Selena Kiser, Bat Conservation International: page 31 (bottom)
Merlin D. Tuttle, Bat Conservation International: pages 4, 6, 7, 9, 10, 13,
    18, 19, 20, 21 (top), 23, 26, 27, 28, 31 (top)
A.N.T. Photo Library/NHPA: page 12
Photo Researchers, Inc.: Gregory G. Dimijian: page 16; Tom McHugh:
    page 21 (bottom); Dr. Merlin Tuttle/BCI: front cover, pages 8, 15;
    Dr. Paul A. Zahl: page 25
Visuals Unlimited: Theo Allofs: page 29; William Beatty: page 14;
    Rick and Nora Bowers: page 22; Joe McDonald: page 17
Other images by Corbis, Corel, and Photodisc

Crabtree Publishing Company

www.crabtreebooks.com   1-800-387-7650

Cataloging-in-Publication Data
Sjonger, Rebecca.
   The life cycle of a bat / Rebecca Sjonger & Bobbie Kalman.
      p. cm. -- (The life cycle series)
   Includes index.
   ISBN-13: 978-0-7787-0671-7 (rlb)
   ISBN-10: 0-7787-0671-0 (rlb)
   ISBN-13: 978-0-7787-0701-1 (pbk)
   ISBN-10: 0-7787-0701-6 (pbk)
   1. Bats--Life cycles--Juvenile literature. I. Kalman, Bobbie. II. Title.
   QL737.C5S58 2005
   599.4--dc22   2005020742
                                                   LC

**Published in
the United States**
PMB16A
350 Fifth Ave.
Suite 3308
New York, NY
10118

**Published
in Canada**
616 Welland Ave.,
St. Catharines, Ontario,
Canada
L2M 5V6

**Published in the
United Kingdom**
73 Lime Walk
Headington
Oxford
OX3 7AD
United Kingdom

**Published
in Australia**
386 Mt. Alexander Rd.,
Ascot Vale (Melbourne)
VIC 3032

Contents

Bats are mammals

Bats are **mammals**. Mammals are **warm-blooded** animals. The bodies of warm-blooded animals stay about the same temperature in both hot and cold places. Mammals breathe air using lungs.

They have backbones, and most have hair or fur on their bodies. Baby mammals drink milk from the bodies of their mothers. About one-quarter of all mammal **species**, or types, are bats!

There are over 1,000 species of bats! The bats above are Wahlberg's epauletted fruit bats.

Two kinds of bats

There are two kinds of bats—**insect-eating bats** and **fruit bats**. Most bats are insect-eating bats. Insect-eating bats have small bodies and eat mainly insects. The bodies of fruit bats are larger than are the bodies of insect-eating bats. Fruit bats eat mainly fruit.

There are over 150 species of fruit bats.

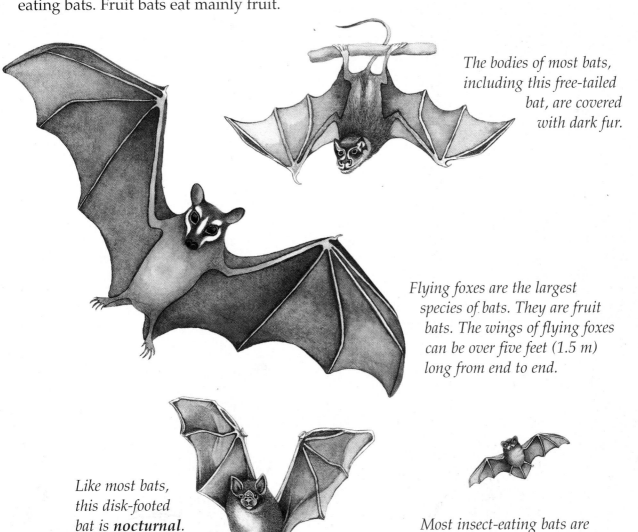

The bodies of most bats, including this free-tailed bat, are covered with dark fur.

Flying foxes are the largest species of bats. They are fruit bats. The wings of flying foxes can be over five feet (1.5 m) long from end to end.

*Like most bats, this disk-footed bat is **nocturnal**. Nocturnal animals are active at night.*

Most insect-eating bats are very small. This thumbless bat is about the same size as a butterfly.

Flying high

These spotted bats are flying in opposite directions.

Bats are the only mammals that can fly. Bats fly to find food and to find safe **roosts**, or shelters. They also fly to escape **predators**. Predators are animals that hunt and eat other animals. Bats can travel long distances by flying high in the sky, where the wind helps carry them along.

Hand-wing

All bats belong to a group of animals called *Chiroptera*. The word "Chiroptera" means "hand-wing." A bat's wings are made of **membrane**, or a thin layer of skin. The membrane is connected to the bat's fingers, arms, legs, and to the sides of its body. The bat moves its wings using its arms and long, thin fingers. Different bats have differently shaped wings.

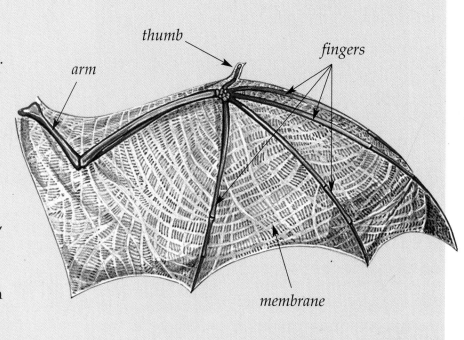

thumb

fingers

arm

membrane

Lift and thrust

When bats fly, they must move
their wings constantly. They
cannot stop flapping their wings
and glide as birds can. Bats lift
their wings to move upward
and **thrust**, or push, them down
to move forward. Bats have
lightweight bodies. If bats were
too heavy, their wings could
not keep them up in the air.

Upside down

Most bats rest by **perching**
upside down from objects.
They hang from surfaces such
as tree branches and rock
walls. Perching upside
down allows bats to take
off quickly when they need
to fly. To take off, bats let go
of the surfaces from which they
are hanging and immediately
flap their wings. Very few bats
can take off from the ground.

This bat is perching upside down. It is ready to let go of the branch and fly away.

7

Bats around the world

Bats live in every part of the world except Antarctica. Different species of bats live in different **habitats**. A habitat is the natural place where an animal lives. Bat habitats include forests, deserts, and cities.

Within their habitats, most species of bats live in **colonies**, or groups. Bat colonies are different sizes. Some colonies are made up of only a few bats. Others include millions of bats.

Many bats, such as the Gambian epauletted fruit bats above, live in habitats that are warm year round.

Old or New World?

Most species of bats are divided into two groups: "Old World bats" and "New World bats." These names refer to the places in which the bats live. The Old World includes Europe, Asia, Africa, and Australia. Old World bats live only on these **continents**. New World bats live only in North America and South America. Some bat species are found in both the Old World and the New World.

The lesser short-nosed fruit bat is an Old World fruit bat. It lives in Southeast Asia.

Bats in North America

Over 40 species of bats live in North America. These bats are mainly insect-eating bats. Some of the most common North American bats are little brown bats, hoary bats, and silver-haired bats. You may see some of these bats flying around your neighborhood after dark!

Silver-haired bats are found all over North America when the weather is warm.

What is a life cycle?

Every animal goes through a set of changes called **life cycle**. First, an animal is born or hatches from an egg. It then grows and changes until it becomes **mature**, or an adult. An adult animal can **mate**, or join together with another adult to make babies. With each baby, a new life cycle begins.

Life span

An animal's life cycle is not the same as its **life span**. An animal's life span is the length of time the animal lives. Different species of bats have different life spans. Large fruit bats, such as the ones shown above, live for about fifteen years in the wild. Smaller insect-eating bats can live for over 30 years in the wild.

The life cycle of a bat

The life cycle shown below is that of a little brown bat. The life cycle begins when a **pup**, or baby bat, is born in early summer. The pup **nurses**, or drinks milk from its mother's body, until it is able to find food on its own. Little brown bats grow quickly!

In about three weeks, the bat pups are fully grown, but they are not yet mature. Most female little brown bats are mature by early fall. Male little brown bats take longer to complete their life cycles. They are not mature until the following summer.

newborn bat pup

three-week-old bat

mature bat

Nursery colonies

Pregnant bats are female bats that are carrying babies inside their bodies. The babies **gestate**, or grow and develop inside the bodies of their mothers. Female bats are pregnant for two to eight months, depending on the species.

Pregnant females usually leave their home roosts and join other female bats to live in larger roosts. These groups of female bats are called **nursery colonies**.

A nursery colony, shown above, can be made up of hundreds of thousands of bat mothers and pups!

Bat pups

Pregnant bats give birth to their pups in the nursery colonies. Most female bats give birth to one pup each year. Many species of bat pups are born without fur, and their eyes are closed. A newborn pup is completely helpless. For the first few days of its life, it clings to its mother's body. The pup nurses several times a day, as shown below.

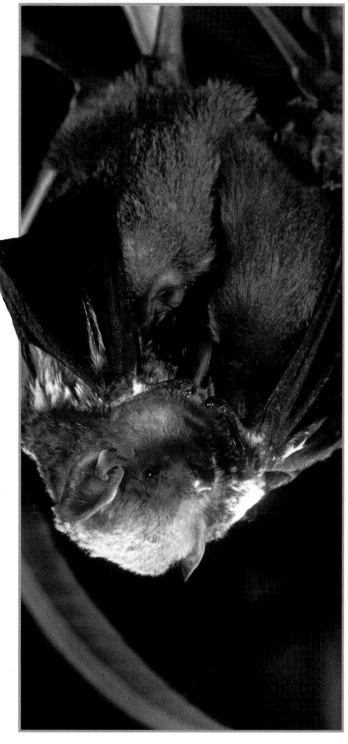

Some bats, such as the red bat above, often give birth to twin pups. In a few bat species, females give birth to as many as four pups at a time.

Growing up

In most bat species, a mother cares for her newborn pup and does not leave it for several days. Then it is time for the mother bat to find food. She leaves her pup with all the other pups in one part of the roost. The pups huddle together to keep warm.

Finding her pup

The mother bat returns often to the roost so her pup can nurse. To locate her pup among the thousands of other pups, the mother bat makes a certain call and then listens for her pup to return the call. Some scientists believe that each pup has a slightly different smell that also helps a mother bat locate her pup.

A room of their own

Mother bats feed their nursing pups in the roost. They do not live with the pups, however. The mothers live with one another in a different part of the roost.

As they grow up, bat pups often spend time playing together. These little brown bat pups are exploring the roost.

Learning to fly

At about three weeks of age, many pups are fully grown. Their wings are strong, and the pups start learning how to fly. Most pups can fly by the time they are four weeks old. Bats learn to fly early in their lives because they are safer when they are flying than when they are perching. When bats are perching, it is easier for predators to catch them. Once the pups learn to fly, they are able to find food for themselves. Before long, the pups are ready to leave the nursery colony.

The bachelor life

Bats that are not part of nursery colonies live in colonies of their own. These colonies are called **bachelor colonies**. Most bachelor colonies are made up of fully grown male pups and mature male bats. Some bachelor colonies also include fully grown female pups.

Making babies

Different bat species are mature and able to mate at different times of the year. When mature male bats are ready to mate, they make certain sounds that tell the females where to find them. Some male bats flap their wings in ways that let the females know they are ready to mate. It is usually the male bat that selects a mating partner. Some bat species mate only once each year. Other bat species mate several times a year.

*Mature males and females of some bat species fly together in tight groups called **swarms** before they mate.*

Waiting for spring

After mating, female bats become pregnant. Pregnant females eat a lot of food so the babies inside their bodies can develop and grow. Pregnant bats that live in warm parts of the world can find food year round. Pregnant bats that live in cold areas may have trouble finding food in winter, however. They become pregnant in autumn, but the babies in their bodies grow very little. In spring, the weather is warm and there is plenty of food available for the pregnant bats. The babies inside their bodies now develop and grow quickly. The babies are born in the spring.

Hanging in the roost

A roost is a place where bats live. Every bat has a roost in which it hangs upside down and rests. Some roosts are small. A small roost may be home to only one bat or a small colony of bats. Other roosts are large. A large roost may shelter a colony that is made up of thousands of bats.

Some bats make roosts in hollow parts of trees. Others make roosts in leaves or in spider webs. Many species of bats make roosts in caves or in structures built by people, including bridges, empty mines, and buildings. The pallid bats shown below are roosting in a shed.

Bats make roosts in sheltered spots that are safe from predators. The roosts are usually located near places where the bats find food.

Roost, sweet roost

Some bats stay in their roosts for only a few days. For example, bats that make roosts in leaves move often. Large colonies of bats that have roosts in caves may use just one roost for their entire lives. In fact, some roosts are home to many **generations** of bat colonies.

Tent-making bats, such as these white fruit bats, create "tents" by nibbling away the centers of leaves.

Super-sized colonies

Very large colonies of bats need large roosts in which to live. Bracken Cave in Texas is the roost for the largest known colony of bats. This roost is home to a nursery colony of about 20 million Mexican free-tailed bats. The colony gathers in this roost every summer.

Male Mexican free-tailed bats live in smaller roosts around Bracken Cave.

Bat food

Most insect-eating bats are **carnivores**. Carnivores are animals that eat other animals. Almost three-quarters of bat species eat insects. Some bats eat up to 2,000 insects in one night! Mosquitoes, beetles, and cockroaches are just a few of the insects that bats eat. Some insect-eating bats also eat other animals. Heart-nosed bats, such as the one shown left, are insect-eating bats that eat birds and fish, as well as insects.

Plant foods

Fruit bats are **herbivores**. Herbivores are animals that eat mainly plant foods. Fruit bats are attracted to foods that taste sweet. They eat fruits such as figs, papayas, and passion fruits. These bats may also eat the **nectar** and **pollen** that are found inside flowers.

Built for eating

If you look closely at a bat's body, you may be able to guess what kind of foods the bat eats. Bats that collect nectar from deep inside flowers have long tongues and snouts. You can see the long tongue of the Mexican long-tongued bat, shown right. Fruit bats have strong teeth for tearing into thick-skinned fruits. Other bats have sharp claws. They use their claws to snatch fish out of water and to carry the fish away.

Vampire bats

Did you believe that all bats drink blood? In fact, only three species of bats drink blood. They are the common vampire bat, the white-winged vampire bat, and the hairy-legged vampire bat. These three species live in Central America and South America. They are the only **parasitic** mammals. A parasitic animal feeds off another living animal's body.

These bats are common vampire bats. They feed off blood from other animals.

Ready for winter

Many bat habitats are in places where the weather is always warm. Bats that live in these habitats can stay in the same roosts year round. Other bat habitats are in places that have cold winters. In winter, there is little food available for bats. Bats that live in cold places must either **migrate** or **hibernate** to survive.

Taking a trip

Animals that migrate move from one place to another when the seasons change. In autumn, migrating bats fly to warm places to find food. Some species may fly all the way from Canada to Mexico or even farther south! The bats return to their home roosts when the weather warms up in spring.

Time-out!

Some bats hibernate instead of migrating. Animals that hibernate go into a deep sleep during the cold winter months. In summer and early fall, bats that hibernate eat a lot of food to add fat to their bodies. They live off the extra fat during winter. Hibernating bats do not leave their roosts for months!

Hibernacula

The winter roosts where bats hibernate are called **hibernacula**. Hibernacula are often found in caves or even attics! Bats must not be disturbed in their hibernacula! If hibernating bats are driven out of their winter roosts, they usually die from the cold weather or starve from the lack of food.

These gray bats are huddled together to keep warm throughout the winter.

Super senses!

Bats have the same five senses that humans have: taste, touch, smell, hearing, and sight. All these senses are well developed in bats. Most bats also possess a sense called **echolocation**. Bats use their senses to find food and to escape predators.

Echoes in the night

Insect-eating bats and a few fruit bats find food at night. They use echolocation to guide them as they fly in the dark.

To echolocate, a bat makes clicking sounds using its tongue, or high-pitched sounds using its **larynx**. These sounds bounce off objects and travel back to the bat as **echoes**. Echoes are waves of sound. When the echoes bounce back to the bat's ears, they create a picture in the bat's brain of the objects in the bat's path. With the help of echolocation, bats can fly in total darkness without hitting objects such as tree branches.

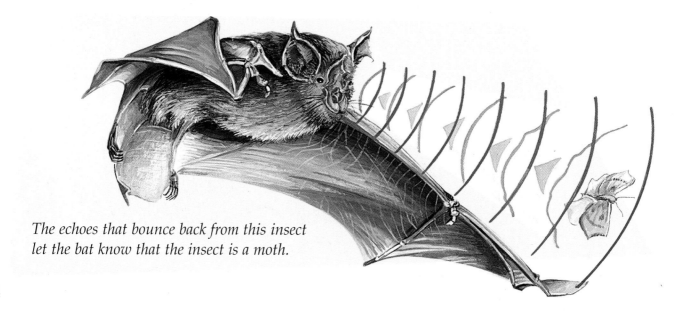

The echoes that bounce back from this insect let the bat know that the insect is a moth.

See and sniff

Most fruit bats are active during the day. They do not need echolocation to guide them. Daytime bats have large eyes and excellent vision. Many fruit bats also have a good sense of smell. They catch the scents of ripe fruits when they are searching for food.

I heard that!

Bats have excellent hearing. They can hear even the quietest sounds. A good sense of hearing helps bats find tiny insects that are hidden in plants or on the ground. It also helps bats avoid being caught by predators that are moving around near the bat.

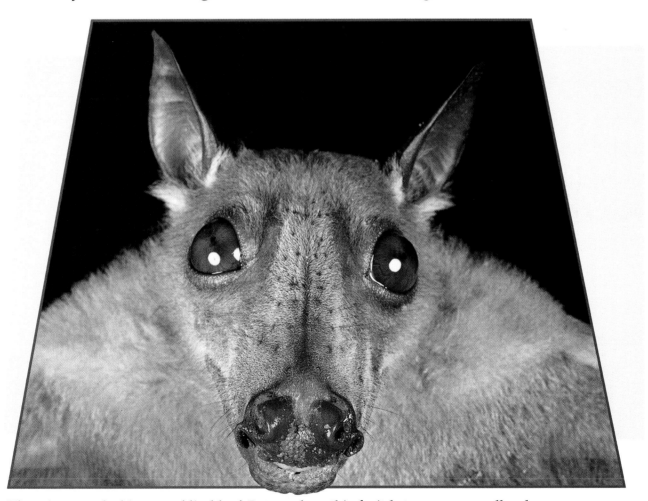

There is no such thing as a blind bat! Bats such as this fruit bat can see as well as humans can see.

Nature's helpers

Bats may be small animals, but they can make a big difference in their habitats! Some bats help plants grow. Bats also help by controlling the **populations** of insects in their habitats.

Pollen movers

Some bats land on flowers as they search for pollen, fruits, or insects to eat. When they touch the flowers, pollen rubs onto their bodies. When the bats move from flower to flower, they carry the pollen with them. Moving pollen from one plant to another is called **pollination**. Pollination allows flowers to make seeds, and seeds grow into new plants. By moving pollen, bats help plants grow.

As this lesser long-nosed bat drinks nectar, it leaves pollen from another saguaro cactus on this cactus.

Spreading seeds

Fruit bats help plants by spreading seeds around their habitats. When a bat eats a fruit, it often carries the fruit away from the area in which it was found. The bat later drops the fruit's seeds on the ground in its waste. New plants often grow where the bat drops the seeds. Many rain-forest plants, including mangoes, cashews, bananas, and figs, need bats to help spread their seeds.

Insect control

Bats help humans by controlling the populations of insects. Insects that bite humans and other animals, as well as insects that eat **crops**, are often considered to be pests. When bats eat pest insects, fewer people are bothered by them. Insect-eating bats can eat hundreds or even thousands of insects in one night!

When bats eat figs and move the seeds, they can increase the number of fig trees in an area.

Dangers to bats

Many bat species are **endangered**. Endangered animals are at risk of dying out in the wild places where they live. At least ten bat species are already **extinct**. Extinct animals no longer exist on Earth. The populations of over half of all the bats living in North America are getting smaller.

Why are bats in trouble?

In most bat species, each female gives birth to only one pup a year. When the number of bats that are born each year is fewer than the number of bats that die each year, the bat population decreases. Many bats die from **natural causes** such as diseases. Some bats die from causes that people can prevent, however. **Habitat loss**, pollution, and **interrupted hibernation** are all dangers to bats that people can prevent.

The Marianas flying fox, shown above, is an endangered bat. It is at risk of dying out in the wild.

Habitat loss

Forests around the world are home to many bats. Some of the forests in which bats live are threatened by companies that cut down all the trees in an area. When the trees are removed, bat roosts and sources of food are removed, too. Without their habitats, most bat colonies do not survive.

Stop pollution!

Many bat habitats are also destroyed by pollution. Pollution harms the plants, soil, air, and water in an area, leaving bats with unhealthy food and damaged homes. You can help stop pollution, however. Ask your parents to stop using chemicals on their lawns and gardens. Walk or ride your bicycle instead of driving. Dispose of garbage properly, remembering always to reduce, reuse and recycle. By doing these simple things, you can help protect the habitats of bats and many other animals.

Help bats!

The more you know about bats, the better prepared you will be to help them. Find out which bat species live near your home. Look on the Internet and read more bat books to find out what bats eat, when they are most active, and when you are most likely to see them.

Once you know more about bats, you can begin to think of ways you can help them. You might ask your family and friends not to bother bats in their winter roosts—even if the bats are in their attics! Interrupting the hibernation of bats can cause the bats to die.

Spread the word

Some people kill bats because they mistakenly believe that bats spread diseases or that bats are dangerous. A few bats may indeed spread diseases, but no more so than many other animals. Bats bite only to defend themselves, and true vampire bats rarely have contact with people. Tell people who are scared of bats the truth about these animals!

Vampire bats are very gentle animals. They take only small amounts of blood from other animals and rarely hurt them.

Bat houses

Bat houses are **artificial**, or human-made, roosts. Your community can set up bat houses to provide bats with safe places to live. It is important to educate people about bats. Teach people that bat houses may help with insect control by attracting more bats to the area. Be patient when you first put up your bat house! It may be a while before bats find it and use it as a roost. If you are buying a bat house, make sure it is approved by Bat Conservation International. Check out their website at www.batcon.org to learn more about bat houses.

Glossary

Note: Boldfaced words that are defined in the text may not appear in the glossary.

continent One of seven large areas of land on Earth

crops Plants grown by people for food

generation One step in the history of a family; a mother bat and her pup are two generations

habitat loss The shrinking of natural areas of land where animals live and find food because of human activity

interrupted hibernation Deep sleep that is disturbed, which may cause an animal to die

larynx The body part a mammal uses to speak or make noise; also called the voice box

natural causes Usual or normal reasons for an animal to die

nectar A sweet liquid in flowers

nursery colony A large group of mother bats and their pups that live together

perching Resting on a tree branch or other surface

pollen A powdery substance in flowers that plants need to make new flowers

population The total number of a species living in a certain area

roost A shelter in which bats live

Index

1 2 3 4 5 6 7 8 9 0 Printed in the U.S.A. 4 3 2 1 0 9 8 7 6 5